$ 50.00 OFF ANY ONE OF MY LIVE  **SEMINARS! EMAIL ME AT** <u>odbhservices@yahoo.com</u>

" There is no hunting like the hunting of man, and those who have done it long enough and liked it, never care for anything else thereafter."
- Ernest Hemmingway

This is my first book published, more to come!

Kelly

This book is dedicated to the memory of Special Agent Wade Andrew Reader who was tragically killed off duty on March 10, 2010. We miss you "Billy Bob" but we know your smiling over us and

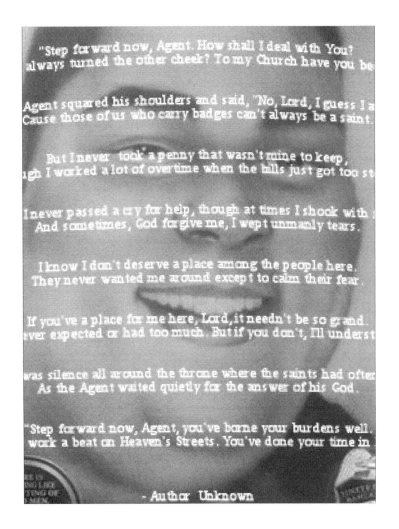

BRIEF HISTORY ON BOUNTY HUNTERS

Bounty Hunters date back as far as you can imagine. From the beginning of civilization there were rewards for people to be brought in front of a tribunal or court of some sort. With law enforcement as vague as it was, vigilante justice was predominantly the way things were handled.

As the civilized world progressed, so did law enforcement and the structure of the bail system.

With this is mind, you must first understand exactly what bail is.

Bail is essentially the insurance of a defendant charged with a crime to appear before the court and allows the defendant the chance to live his or her life without being incarcerated but still "technically" in custody.

As you have likely seen in the old cowboy movies "WANTED! DEAD or ALIVE", those days are long gone and now this is an industry of being safe and returning the wanted back to custody without any harm.

Some of the first real bounty hunters that would be known in modern day would be the Pinkerton's. I am sure you have heard of Pinkerton Security & Investigations, this firm at one time was the largest security & investigation firm in the world; but over the years with monetary issues they have faded away. The Pinkerton's would go after bounty's all over the country and became known for ALWAYS HAVING AN EYE ON WHATS GOING ON, hence their logo has a seeing eye in it, and the term "Private Eye" derived from. In all reality the Pinkerton's are the ones who pioneered this industry.

The easiest way to explain the job of a Bail Enforcement Agent is this. Take the United States Marshals Service; this is the closest thing to being a Marshal without being a sworn law enforcement officer; what are the USMS known for? Catching fugitives as are bounty hunters, only remember bounty hunters have much more leeway than that of a federal marshal as they are sworn law enforcement officers and a bounty hunter is a private citizen acting as a duly authorized AGENT of the bondsman to insure that the contractual obligations of the bail bond are in fact enforced.

With that being said, your are essentially an insurance investigator with the power of arrest.

And of course over the years there has always been negative publicity on this profession we have chose to work in; but seldom is it heard the positive aspect of the bail enforcement profession such as:

In 2003 over 52,000 fugitives from justice were apprehended by bail enforce red nationwide at NO COST TO THE TAXPAYERS

That NO BAIL ARREST BY A BAIL ENFORCER is paid for by the taxpayer as it is a private contract between the bondsman and agent

As previously stated these are important things to know especially for Public Relations sake and you want to keep good P.R. within the industry as that is what keeps you employed.

Remember just as in the old days of the wild west, you too are working to make money. You don't catch your fugitive, you don't get paid. No body, No bounty. It's as simple as that.

BAIL BONDSMAN'S RIGHT TO ARREST

The Decision of the United States Supreme Court TAYLOR v TAINTOR 16 WALL 366, 1872 is the single most important law to know; as it is your governing arrest authority granted by the US SUPREME COURT.

" SUCH IS NOW THE SETTLED RULE: WHEN BAIL IS GIVEN, THE PRINCIPAL IS REGARDED AS DELIVERED TO THE CUSTODY OF HIS SURETIES (BAIL BONDSMAN). THEIR DOMINION IS A CONTINUANCE OF THE ORIGINAL IMPRISONMENT. WHENEVER THEY CHOOSE TO DO SO THEY MAY SEIZE HIM AND DELIVER HIM UP IN THEIR DISCHARGE; AND IF THAT CANNOT BE DONE AT ONCE, THEY MAY IMPRISON HIM UNTIL IT CAN BE DONE. THEY MAY EXERCISE THEIR RIGHTS IN PERSON OR BY "AGENT". THEY MAY PURSUE HIM INTO ANOTHER STATE, MAY ARREST HIM ON THE SABBATH; AND, IF NECESSARY MAY BREAK AND ENTER HIS HOUSE FOR THAT PURPOSE. THE SEIZURE IS NOT MADE BY VIRTUE OF NEW PROCESS. NONE IS NEEDED. IT IS LIKENED TO THE REARREST BY THE SHERIFF OF AN ESCAPING PRISONER."

Learn to know this ruling because it is the single most important thing you need to know as a professional recovery agent. This is what gives you the authority to do your job so ALWAYS keep a copy of this law with you! Most credible identification will have this ruling displayed somewhere on the ID so that is easily accessible to hand to anyone who wishes to question your authority. It's always good to be able to quote the law when questioned by an official and then show them the law on paper, so know it ; learn it ; live it.

As clearly stated in the above decision, you are a direct representative of the bail bondsman and need to act accordingly. Remember not only will your conduct reflect on you and your agency but the bail agent as well; and as you know there is already enough negative publicity on this industry we don't need anymore.

"BREAKING INTO THE HOUSE FOR THAT PURPOSE"

I think I may have only kicked in maybe 16 doors in my career so that tells you what the chances are but just in case I wanted to tell you how to do it and how to NOT get yourself in trouble.

Knock and announce yourself loudly for at least 15 seconds, BE SURE TO HAVE ALL EXITS COVERED; if you know without a doubt that the fugitive is in fact in that building or home and it is on the address listed on the paperwork OR you have chased him to that address and have Law Enforcement there to give the go ahead to boot the door THEN you may kick it. Kick near the lock and doorknob with your knee bent and not to sprain yourself or blow your ACL. If you are smart purchase a fireman's sledge hammer for $ 40 bucks in case of this situation.

Remember you cannot leave the property unsecured as well, every door I have kicked there was drugs or other illegal items that permitted POLICE to have probable cause to go get a search warrant and to stay to secure the scene and the property. So always remember the consequences of your actions, YOU CAN GET SUED or WORSE ARRESTED for it so be sure before you take that step. And its really not something that you or the bondsman wants happening as it again gives that renegade outlook on things.

YOU DO NOT WANT A REPUTATION AS A DOOR KICKER! You want the bondsman to know you for your ability to get the fugitive picked up without incident and he will end up referring you to other bondsman once you establish yourself with him. Remember this is a business of saving liability for you and the client. So be smart.

STATES OUTLAWING COMMERCIAL BAIL

There are several states who have outlawed the commercial bail bond industry and therefore don't want to respect the authority of the recovery agent entering their state to make an apprehension. In some cases this can be a Class D Felony charge.

There are more and more states requiring licensing, and it is YOUR responsibility to keep up to date on these laws.

There is one particular website I recommend www.fugitiverecovery.com this lists all applicable bail laws in every state. Also a great advertising tool! I have personally been assigned cases from agencies that were referred to me by this site.

Check it out it will help in your newfound career!

The TAYLOR v TAINTOR U.S. Supreme Court Decision is in no way the final say so in bail enforcement. You need to find out every state law on bail enforcement and follow their laws to the tee. The states are becoming more and more strict with regards to bail enforcement and remember this as well; we do not get enough positive publicity and rarely do we get recognition for doing a good job. What you usually see is negative publicity and wrong doings of untrained bounty hunters.

A good way of increasing a positive image for bail enforcement is by providing press releases when you make an apprehension. The release should look something like this:

FOR IMMEDIATE RELEASE!

Acme Bail Enforcement made a fugitive apprehension at 4:15 p.m. on Wednesday November 4 on the 1400 block of Anywhere Ave. John Doe wanted for failure to appear on drug charges was apprehended without incident and surrendered to the Anywhere County Jail where he awaits sentencing. Agents John Doe and Mike Doe were the arresting agents in this case. Any questions please email acmebail@email.com or call (123) 456-7890

Short and to the point and lets the public know what a good job you are doing and that we are out and about working. This is important and especially helpful in your advertising efforts as well.

There is no law that states you cannot announce what a good job you have done. In fact it will help the industry as a whole and award you and the industry with positive publicity.

Keep a copy of the state laws that you are operating in with you always! Have them handy as well as Taylor v Taintor with you in case a law enforcement official should question your right to arrest and authority. It is not the fault of the officer he has not been educated in bail enforcement so do him and his department a favor and educate them.

I know of incidents regarding a judge stating that there was no power of arrest by the bail bondsman and the agent showing the exact laws pertaining to that state and Taylor v Taintor to the judge and the judge apologizing on record for the misunderstanding.

See right there shows that the laws are not as familiar as they should be, it's your responsibility to know them so that you can reference them when needed.

NETWORKING AND ASSOCIATIONS

The values of networking are unimaginable. Why spend countless hours and unnecessary money on going out of state when you can contact one of the people in your network from that area? The only time you should go out of state to work is if the bounty is large and/or it is a major case. But why not contact another agent in your network and pay him 40% of the reward to hook him up and meet you half way so you can get your fugitive and take him to the jail and collect your big reward. Common business sense isn't hard, just use your head. You will get experience as well as a little money for helping out on an arrest, if he is professional he will not burn you on the money thing and likewise for you; if you want to make it in this business don't ever burn someone.

If you choose to hire an agent from your network pay him a reasonable fee and have a contract set. You would expect it if the agent contacted you to make the arrest right? Remember your going to make a good amount of money yourself, the last thing you need is a reputation for not paying fair to your contracted agents.

Every time you are out and about and run across a law enforcement officer be sure to introduce yourself and exchange business cards and offer to help him and the department I any way, add to your database of contacts. Be sure to send out Christmas Cards to your contacts to be sure they will remember you and include a business card again. Also you never know when you will have to call upon one of them for assistance and if they already know who you are things will go a lot smoother. When your on vacation be sure to bring an ample supply of business cards and/or promotional materials so that you can make contact with officers out of state or area and be sure to get their cards as well. It really is about who you know in this business.

Associations like the United States Professional Bail Bond Investigators Association (www.bountyhunt.com) give you an ID card, T Shirt and Certificate of Membership for $ 45 a year and post your contact information on a roster. This membership is INVALUABLE as Billy Wells the founder and a friend of mine is one of the greatest bounty hunters ever, and is always available for advice.

There are associations that offer credentials in Spanish, this is especially helpful when working in heavily populated areas of Hispanics, Spanish is the second language of the United States and you will need them.

Associations also help with legal issues at hand in the bail industry, with laws getting more and more strict you want to have someone on your side. But do not believe any association that says you cannot operate without their credentials, that is a bold faced lie. The whole time I was an active field agent I utilized credentials issued to me by the agency I was employed by, and also had generic credentials as back up. So again, beware of any association that states they are the only "approved"

association. Research all the different law enforcement, investigation, bail enforcement etc. associations and join as many as you can, it will help in the long run.

I also strongly recommend that you become a member or associate member of all law enforcement organizations. This will show the law enforcement community that you are trying to work with them and support what they do; but do not make a mistake a lot of agents in the past have done by displaying any law enforcement association on your work vehicle as it will get you into trouble. You do not want to attract attention to your car, remember this is a job that requires you to be inconspicuous and covert the majority of the time. Unless you have a separate vehicle for transporting prisoners then you can display anything within the law you wish. BUT REMEMBER YOUR NOT A COP DON'T TRY AND BE ONE! No need for lights and siren, your not authorized to utilize them so why have them? That is just asking for trouble.

FUGITIVE'S RIGHTS

Essentially when they are bonded out of jail they are the property of the bondsman until they are discharged. But they still have a few basic rights and you need to know that and follow it or risk being sued or worse arrested.

There is no need to be overly aggressive unless the situation warrants it. Be courteous, but in command at all times. No reason to speak to them or treat them harshly.

I have noticed the way the media and television portrays the modern day bail enforcement agent to be an overaggressive, rogue cop want to be; and that is the last thing you want to be known as! There is no reason to push or shove the subject around, especially when they are already in handcuffs; if you are forced to use force on the subject to subdue him only use the amount of force necessary to get him into custody and keep him under control that is it.

If you are dealing with a cooperative subject then there is no reason you can't give him a cigarette or soda; if you are traveling with a prisoner over a long period of time you are required to give bathroom breaks as well as meals; here are a few key points to remember when doing so:

- When possible try and find a restroom in private, if unavailable take to rest stop cover cuffs with a shirt or something take them into restroom facilities after your partner has checked for weapons etc. Once exited the restroom conduct a thorough search on subject.
- If transporting a prisoner of opposite sex you should ALWAYS have a member of same sex with you for restroom and searches.
- For meals ALWAYS go through drive thru and get the fugitive something they can eat with their hands.
- ANY prescription medication must be administered as instructed NO OVER THE COUNTER MEDICINE WILL EVER BE ADMINSTERED!

TRAINING, TRAINING, TRAINING!

I know this book may seem redundant, but you will quickly learn that this job is as well. I continue to cover the same subjects just in different aspects of the job.

There are hundreds of training institutes around the United States that offer any type of training you could imagine, chances are most of the training you really need can be obtained relatively close to your home or office or by going through ODBH Training Division. I am going to cover a few recommendations fro agents old and new.

- **CDT NON DEADLY FORCE TRAINING (www.cdt-training.com)** This is an advanced course in defensive tactics. I myself am a former graduate of the system and can't even recall how many times it has saved my behind by applying the techniques properly. The founder of the system is one of America's leading experts on personal security and threat management. The cost may seem relatively expensive at the time but the training will pay itself off especially with all the backing the company has. This training includes a T Shirt and Certificate.
- **ASP Certified Officer Training.** The ASP Baton is synonymous with any type of law enforcement. The cost for the training is surprisingly low and you get a wallet certification card and a one of a kind certificate. The training covers proper usage of the baton as well as carrying etc.
- **CPR/Advanced First Aid.** This is a requirement for ANY AGENT. Again, you never know when something will happen to your partner, your prisoner or the general public and you need to be prepared for any situation.
- **Interview and Interrogation.** There are two schools in which I am a graduate of and recommend as the best in the world. Wicklander-Zelowski and The Reid Method. Both are fantastic schools and I recommend taking both courses in your career.
- **Report Writing.** You need to know the key components to a good report and this is an important factor in every case.

You want your client to be 100% trusting in you to recover their bond. You should have copies of all certifications, your social security card, drivers license, and next of kin information etc. In a file for them and hand it to them upon receiving cases from them for their file.

Just because you have completed this course does not mean your going to walk out and get work right away. You need to use common sense, contact local bondsman and ask if you can apprentice FOR FREE under them and their recovery agents. Two or Three days a month isn't going to hurt you, and if you prove yourself as a valuable asset you will get hired on. Most of the time the Recovery Agents will flip you $ 20-$50 or more for assisting in an investigation and arrest IF you are actually assisting.

Take Notes!!!! When working under a seasoned agent don't be afraid to ask questions and take notes, matter of fact if your not doing those things they will not take you seriously.

Always have some form of photography equipment whether cell phone camera or digital camera with you. You want to take a pic of your fugitive in custody for your records and records of the bondsman.

NEVER work alone. ALWAYS have a partner. There should be no need for an explanation in this situation. SAFETY FIRST. ALWAYS USE YOUR INSTINCT and KNOW YOUR ENVIORNMENT!!!

Brush up on your computer skills. The internet is your new friend. And not for fun but for research. Majority of the time on a case is spent researching online. This job is 90% boredom, 10% action. You will spend majority of time at home or in an office researching information on the fugitive.

Contact your local college that offers a police academy and find out if there are sub courses that you can take that will further advance your skills.

It would be wise to go to your local Police Department/Sheriff and introduce yourself to them. While your there be sure to stress the importance of trained investigators and exchange business cards and offer to help their department in anyway possible. Familiarize yourself with the officers in the Fugitive or Warrants Division and get to know them, they are the ones that you will utilize.

If you are known in the departments then they will be more likely to help you then if you were coming off the street. Familiarize yourself with proper terminology in the law enforcement community, know your role is an important one, but never try and look, act or dress like a police officer as it will only discredit you and the organization you are employed by. The usual dress for an agent is plainclothes with a badge/id around the neck and/or a "raid jacket" as I have discussed in the classroom. NEVER FLASH A BADGE AT A POLICE OFFICER!!!!!!!!!!!!!!!!!!!!!!! IDENTIFY YOURSELF VERBALLY AND BY DISPLAYING CREDENTIALS!!!! They could care less about a badge they want to see official identification that will ensure them they are working with a professional and not some rogue cop want to be like on television.

The biggest problem with this business is everybody wants to do it because of television hype and most are cowboys and cop want to bees. Simple fact of the matter they are the ones that get hurt, killed or arrested. Never act ignorant in the field, remember when you are working there are more eyes on you then you know. Acting ignorant and foolish will destroy any credibility you may have, remember do it better and cleaner than the last guy because your performance could make or break the next agent that comes to that area; and if that department has had problems with agents in the past, ensure them by your performance that all agents are not like that and the majority of agents are well trained. ALWAYS send a letter of thanks to the department and officers that assisted you.

Last and one of the most important things, DON'T DO ANYTHING ILLEGAL!!!!!! There is no reason for you to have a siren or flashing lights in your vehicle as an agent, you can't use them and it would be illegal for you to do so. You are not a police officer remember that, you don't need a look alike scout car, and you want to be covert so use your head. I cannot stress the importance of this matter enough, never attempt to identify yourself as a law enforcement officer! The last thing you want to do is be hemmed up with an impersonation charge, and know the state rules and regulations for badges, patches and other means of identification as you do not want to violate these rules either.

PREREQUISITES FOR EMPLOYMENT AS A BAIL ENFORCEMENT AGENT

There are not that many prerequisites for working as an agent; but the ones that are prominent I will cover as you cannot function without these basic skills:

Basic understanding of the functions of a computer
Working knowledge of the internet and how to utilize the internet in investigations
Basic understanding pf phone skills
PATIENCE
Verbal skills both in person and on the phone
Ability to read, write and speak English fluently.

When you reading this manual, write down questions and email me!

The worst thing I have seen is someone paying the money to go through an academy or training course and have no understanding of what they are learning.

As you were told in grade school, there is no stupid question! Especially in this field there are so many things that are difficult and unique and ever changing that when you first get into this field you will quickly realize it can be overwhelming, ask and learn as much as you can. The best thing for you to do is to write down questions during your instruction and ask at end of class or at breaks if they haven't been resolved.

GEAR THAT YOU WILL WANT TO ACCUMULATE OVER YOUR CAREER

I am a firm believer that if you dress for success, you will be successful. With that in mind this is what I recommend for agents to wear. There are casual tactical pants called 5.11 Gear around $ 40.00, get khaki color as it is less aggressive of a tone; they may be a little expensive but hook up a pair of boots and a polo and you will look very professional in the field.

8" Zippered Police Style Boots $ 40-$ 200, you mine as well buy them because whether it be a snowy day or rainy day or sunny and humid these boots will protect your feet and are a good choice for a professional look. MAKE SURE THEY ARE WATERPROOF!!! And while your at it, get some thermal socks for in the winter, you'll thank me when your in the cold, DO NOT GET STEEL TOES trust me you will regret it.

A complete duty belt, $ 100-$ 500, a duty belt can be leather or nylon, I recommend nylon for the durability. It should contain the appropriate holster for the gear you carry.

A Laptop Computer $ 200-$ 2,000 this is a luxury but will become a necessity if you don't have a Smartphone. Get a wireless card and be online anywhere you go.

Hidden Agenda Jacket $ 70-$ 200, a little pricey but an awesome accessory to have as it can be used in summer and winter.

Taser, $ 600-$1500, it is an invaluable tool and I recommend this as a priority over having a firearm.

A "Posse" box to keep your file in when your at a home or business and has forms and such in it that you will fill so that you can hand out to Law Enforcement or unruly persons.

A portable file box to keep your open case files in; YOU ALWAYS SHOULD HAVE YOUR OPEN CASES WITH YOU! Keep a spare set of handcuffs or disposable restraints in your box in case you spot a fugitive while out and about.

ITEMS YOU WILL NEED RIGHT AWAY!
2 SETS OF HANDCUFFS
FLASHLIGHT
BADGE/ID CARD

ITEMS THAT YOU NEED TO GET AS SOON AS POSSIBLE

O/C SPRAY
BATON
LEG IRONS
BODY ARMOR
RECHARGEABLE FLASHLIGHT

**** NOTE TO STUDENT:

WE OFFER ALL THESE ITEMS AND MORE JUST CONTACT US FOR A CATALOG!

A good briefcase and duffle bag to keep your gear and documents in. The gear bag should be big enough for the following:

2 Days worth of clothes for the season
Hygiene Products
All Gear
Any extra paperwork needed
4 bottles of water
Pain Reliever
MRE's (Trust me you will need them)

I recommend learning Spanish as a tool for your survival. Go through Rosetta Stone as they are who we use for foreign language tasking.

Must have a cell phone! Make sure you have enough minutes on your plan for the job, set up voicemail, DO NOT STATE YOU'RE AN AGENT on the voicemail. A camera phone is always recommended.

MAKING YOUR AGENCY

This is a bit tricky; SO let's jump right in. Unless you have a registered business license with the entity you plan on using listed, or a DBA (doing business as) you should avoid these titles for your agency. U.S., UNITED STATES, BUREAU or FEDERAL. These titles can be confused with Official Government Agencies and will likely get you into trouble. Becoming an LLC or INC is always an option, while expensive the benefits are crucial.

Now, for the dreaded word, INSURANCE. There are only a handful of companies who will insure a recovery agent simply because of the high risk position. Truth is you need liability insurance, most reputable bonding agencies will not hire you without it. I also recommend PRE PAID LEGAL SERVICES.

First of all I worked out of my home with a PO BOX or a UPS STORE BOX as a physical address. One is safety, two is expense. What is the purpose of having an office if your going to be gone in the field chasing bad guys right? Most of the time the bondsman will allow you to use their office anyways.

Advertising is all in your own hands. www.vistaprint.com you figure out the rest.

LAW ENFORCEMENT RELATIONS

Dealing with law enforcement will be an everyday occurrence with your position of becoming a bail enforcer. So get used to it quick. Learn the lingo and always be courteous and respectful and thank the officers for their assistance. I still send out thank you cards and certificates of recognition to departments who have went above and beyond to help, it goes along way.

Law enforcement officers are a different breed of people plain and simple; they want things done their way and their way only and they don't like to be told what to do by an outsider so remember that. As previously stated in class they are likely going to have information on your fugitive and probably have dealt with him before so remember they are here to help you. When requested I have had police backup 99.9% of the time, the only time they would not send back up is when they were tied up with calls or against department policy. Other than that if you have all your paperwork squared away, and act professional you will have no issues getting assistance from Law Enforcement.

Some of the agents I have worked with have conducted themselves so professionally that they were invited to sit in the war room and drink coffee while the police went and got their fugitive for them and brought him or her back to them so they could take them in, I have seen police officers tell me to jump in and I would go with them for their shift and would scour the area looking for the fugitive. There was one police department that I went to quite often and every time we would go there and we called them to have someone meet us at the station they would always be glad to see us because they knew us from working in the area so much, they would have pizza or whatever in the break room and would tell us to go get something to eat and chill for a while why they would help us look for information through their computers. Once you make a good impression on an agency your set just don't screw it up. I was working a case on the east coast where two uniformed officers came and asked my partner and I how we were doing and said it's funny how professional you are, just three months ago they had some "bounty hunters" kick a door in, cuff a guy and take him in their car, the mother called the police stating three men in all black with masks broke into her house and kidnapped her son, these guys were spotted just down the road and a felony stop with guns drawn and all was done. The paperwork was all legitimate and they were all licensed to carry firearms and all, but had no identification showing on them no badge, patch nothing. Their names and ID's were recorded and they were told to never come back to that city and that is a big city and an active city at that. These "bounty hunters", not professional recovery agents made the whole industry look bad by not checking in with the police, breaking down doors and acting like Rambo when they should have known better, this is what happens when there is no training involved. I was fortunate enough to teach many future agents during my career and I always stressed the importance of not dressing like SWAT! There are some circumstances that warrant it, very few. But just use common sense and you will have no problems.

DEALING WITH A BAD ARREST

There will be a time when a friendly customer (this is a joke) will attempt to either sue you or be a defendant in a drug case which you helped make or break, whatever the case may be where you will be subpoenaed for court and have to testify. I am going to go over the basics for everyone to know, just in case your ever in this predicament.

What to wear: Different strokes for different folks. I have worn everything from a suit and tie with my badge displayed around my neck to khakis and a polo with the badge patch on left breast; to each their own, see what is legal in your area before donning anything resembling a uniform, the last thing you want to do is get arrested for impersonating a police officer!

When arriving at a courthouse, BRING THE WHOLE FILE YOU HAVE ON THE FUGITIVE AND BRING A COMPLETE COPY FOR THE PROSECUTOR!!!!!!!!! All your field notes should be typed up upon completion of the case and signed and dated at the bottom of each page. All this information will be needed and also this will allow you to refer back to your records of the arrest. Check in with the prosecutors office upon arrival and hand the report to the prosecutor that is handling the case personally. Be sure to have copies of your credentials in the file for their records. Be respectful to everyone! Yes mam and no sir is going to get you a long way.

Do not leave the courthouse without first checking in with the prosecutor first! And if your going to lunch or whatever case may be, make sure the prosecutor has your cell phone number to reach you right away.

You may be called to do a deposition and you will need to be sure you have all your facts about the case in order, ANY TIME you are called into court or interviewed by an attorney you need to have all your facts straight be sure to review the case before you go to the hearing or meeting. The defense attorney will ALAWAYS try and trip you up so be prepared and stick to your story remember you have the upper hand whether you think so or not. Remember also, the prosecution is counting on you to help close the case.

CONFIDENTIAL INFORMANTS

Confidential Informants means just that CONFIDENTIAL! You should never reveal your source of information! A C.I. can be anyone from a neighbor to a relative and the last thing you want to do is have the informant get back to your fugitive and harm come upon your informant.

I have used everything from a kid on the street to a prostitute, I had one incident where a known prostitute who I had used for information in the past was walking down the road and I was looking for a guy who was in her area, I pulled up, let her get in my car since it was winter and I could see she was freezing, I am not here to judge anyone just to get my job done is what I told her and for a measly $ 20 she would tell me anything I needed to know, she never dressed trashy like imagined, she dressed for the season not in the best clothes but well enough. We drove about 3 blocks and I asked her if she wanted a coffee, she did so I stopped at the store got two cups of coffee and we pulled around side of store so no one would see her talking to me, I was showing her the fugitives photo and the area he is supposed to be in; when two uniformed officers walked up with weapons drawn ordering us out of the car, we did so cooperatively and the officer began telling me I was going to be under arrest for soliciting a prostitute, I then asked him to pull my credentials and badge out of my jacket pocket and that I had weapons on me as I was on the job as a recovery agent and he is putting my informant in danger as well as my cover. He released me after verifying who I was and asked if there was anything they could do, I gave them a wanted poster and was on my way. Just like that could have been killed, cover blown and informant never to trust me again. This is 100% the fault of local dispatch who did not notify officers I was in the area, or the officers didn't listen.

Informants are fueled by three things generally, money, revenge and a moral obligation. I have had people lead me right to the fugitive and wanted over $ 100 bucks to do it, but it was worth it. I have had some do it because they were screwed over by the fugitive and I have used known drug dealers to help me to "rid the competition". Everybody plays a roll, its your job to figure out if that roll will help you.

WHAT TO DO WHEN YOU GET YOUR FIRST CASE FROM A BONDSMAN

Ask for all paperwork that the bondsman has on the fugitive and always try and get a picture. Next review the case AT THE Bondsman's OFFICE!!! Scan through each page and if there are things missing you need ask the bondsman for the items.

These are the documents you must have to make a lawful arrest:

NOTARIZED AUTHORIZATION TO ARREST DEFENDANT ON A BAIL BOND

COPIES OF BAIL AGREEMENT
COPY OF ACTUAL BOND
COPY OF BAIL BOND APPLICATION

Anything else you are able to get such as a CERTIFIED copy of the warrant are a luxury.

Go to your work station from there. Get online and check everything from Face book to Email accounts that may be the fugitives. I am not going to tell you the sites that will do the job for you , but you will figure it out.

Call the indemnitor (CO SIGNER) and start questioning them, they know they are responsible for the money and be sure to tell them that they are going to lose everything if the bondsman has to sue them for it on top of your costs, the attorney costs and the cost of the bond is going to run them 5 times the amount of the bond.

Call every number listed and use different pretexting tricks, be a telemarketer, or a phone service etc. Try and get some intelligence on your skip that way.

If you get stuck on a case feel free to email me at odbhservices@yahoo.com and I will do all I can to assist you.

OTHER JOBS TO SUBSIDIZE YOUR INCOME WHILE GETTING STARTED

**SECURITY OFFICER
LOSS PREVENTION STORE DETECTIVE
PROCESS SERVICE
EXECUTIVE/DIGNITARY PROTECTION
  SERVICES**

PRIVATE INVESTIGATOR
INTELLIGENCE ANALYST
INTELLIGENCE FIELD OPERATIVE
REPOSSESSION AGENT

FILING A POLICE COMPLAINT IN THE COURSE OF YOUR DUTY

There may come a time in your career where you will have to file a police complaint on the fugitive or someone other than the fugitive you are arresting. I am going go cover a few of the scenarios and how to handle it the way I would have done it and the ways that have worked best for me.

WHEN THE FUGITIVE IS APPREHENDED AND THEY ASSUALT YOU, PRESS CHARGES!!!! Be sure to subdue your defendant and drive to a safe location then call 911 and give them the situation report and you need an officer to meet at this location to file a report. BE SURE TO STRESS YOU WANT TO PRESS CHARGES!!!!

ALWAYS HAVE COPIES OF AN INCIDENT REPORT WITH YOU!!!!!!!!!!!!!! The reason being is you will need this in court and it will go a long way.

BE PREPARED TO GO TO COURT FOR THIS!!! They will likely subpoena you and be sure to include any witnesses on the scene that you are aware of. Depending on the severity of the assault you will need to go to ER or call EMS to transport you. **ALWAYS SEEK MEDICAL ATTENTION** when you are assaulted as this will add legitimacy to your complaint.

If filing a complaint on someone other than the fugitive, you will likely be filing the following complaints:

Hindering an Apprehension
Aiding and Abetting
Harboring a Fugitive

Or you may have to file an assault charge on them as well. Remember you are just a private citizen, but acting professionally and having all your ducks in a row will assure you a favored side.

FOLLOW THE LETTER OF THE LAW AS ANYTHING FALSE IN YOUR REPORT IS A CRIME!!!

Whenever you have to file a complaint be sure to contact the prosecuting attorneys office and offer any assistance they may need. A complete copy of your file and all reports would be the best way to start them trusting you and utilizing your assistance.

Always contact your client if you plan on filing a complaint against someone involved in the case! Let them know step by step and be sure they get a copy of your report as soon as possible so that you may keep them advised on everything that is going on. Remember this will affect them as well as they are the ones who hired you in the first place.

MAKING THE ARREST

Whether it be a traditional style "raid" on a house with law enforcement assistance or you and your partner got to a location and your fugitive is there. From a simple DUI to Murder ALWAYS treat the fugitive as if they are dangerous until they are properly restrained! Until they are in custody they are a threat and need to be treated as one.

Be stern and aggressive in your nature when making an arrest and you usually will not have an altercation. I have made a lot of arrests and maybe 20 have truly put up a serious fight, that's where pepper spray and a taser come in. The ones to watch out for are the little people who don't look like they can do much, NEVER

UNDERESTIMATE A FUGITIVES ABILITY TO HARM YOU OR YOUR PARTNER.

MAKING THE ARREST

Upon initial arrest place them in cuffs behind their back and conduct a thorough search, if it is a male have a male search him if a female have a female search her. If no female is available do a quick pat down not to touch her in areas that would suggest sexual contact and let the jail know that a female was not available so they may conduct a more thorough search. If they are being cooperative you may decided to put there hands in front and cuffed, if a long haul is in the future it is a necessity, but you have matter what they were doing. And I generally transported them in the front seat unless I had a caged vehicle which was rare. I recommend calling the dispatcher where you are taking your prisoner and giving them the starting mileage and time of departure and ETA to the jail, and of course calling it in when you arrive with same information and if any incidents occurred, be sure to keep a log of all your stops made and where they were at also if the stop is longer than 15 minutes I recommend you call dispatcher back and advise her or him of what is going on. Once at the jail go to the sally port and ring the buzzer, announce BAIL ENFORCEMENT 1 male or female IN CUSTODY, they will buzz you in, drive in and get out and secure your weapons and your car keys in a locker and then get your prisoner out and take her or him into the holding area for processing. Once all paperwork is done you get your paperwork sign your forms and head out. Pull out and off to the side and fill out your report. And include all paperwork in the file and either go back out to work or call it a night, it's your call.

REMEMBER pepper spray used in a confined area will contaminate the entire area so be prepared to feel the burn.

If you feel threatened, STOP, LOOK, and LISTEN; assess the situation and use your instinct and environment!!! Don't do anything stupid and try and resolve the situation as quickly and with as little force as possible.

WHAT NOT TO DO

There are a few rules that you should understand and NEVER EVER do these things!

1. Never claim you are a law enforcement officer/agent.

2. Never challenge anyone, your there to arrest the fugitive not rumble with others, protect yourself but do not play the role of I authority and I can use it; your still just a private citizen with power of arrest remember that. Although the police will usually back you up remember they are watching you just as closely as they are watching everyone else.

3. Never ever harm a child! There is no reason for you to ever have to get physical with a minor and if you do plan on going to jail and/or getting sued.

4. Report unsafe living conditions to the authorities, I have made arrests in places that I wouldn't let my dog live and I will tell you after I had my fugitive in custody I made a phone call to the proper authorities.

5. Never claim to be a representative of any court, law enforcement or government agency.

6. Always and I mean ALWAYS identify yourself properly. That means verbally and by showing credentials. Most people will assume you are a law enforcement officer/agent and it is your responsibility to identify yourself properly. I have known numerous people who have been charged with impersonation of a law enforcement officer/agent because they were not identified properly.

7. Never use title or wear any item of clothing with the title of any law enforcement agency on it. I knew one guy who tried using the title "Special Police" I do not know what he was thinking, I do know he wasn't trained properly and never completed an academy and also served time for that charge as well as lost his weapons permits and his vehicle was confiscated. So as you can see the law enforcement community feels very strongly about certain things and it's the law so follow the letter of the law and you will be ok.

8. Never do anything that is illegal, never drink alcohol while working and of course never use any type of narcotic whether it be prescription or illegal no mater what. When you are working a lot of things can happen and you can be assured that if an incident occurs where you use a weapon or are involved in a motor vehicle accident a blood test will be taken to see if you were under the influence of any type of drug or alcohol.

Anything else I would recommend you use common sense and if you have questions about what you can do, then ask before you do it; DON'T TAKE CHANCES!

DON'T BE A SHOW OFF

The last thing you want to be is a show off or a loose cannon as you will lose your business and your respect in this industry. Taking risky chances and not following protocol will only cause you grief and will cost you money as well.

The worse thing in this industry is a liability, if you're a liability because you carry a whole cache of weapons and all that good stuff your not going to get work as a person that is an expert in martial arts or weapons training; your going to get work as a person who has quality resources and is a good investigator that's what matters not that you are a marksman or a black belt, the bondsman could care less about that, the bondsman would much rather see the words Investigator Training than Weapons Training.

Another thing the bondsman could care less about is all the equipment you have and if you have a police car and things like that. What the bondsman is interested in is the skills you have as an investigator or the type of computer equipment that you may have that will increase your ability to track down a fugitive.

Don't be overzealous when working with a law enforcement agency, the best way to describe how to deal with them is this; make them think they have full command over the situation but be authorities in your presence and take charge and set up the planning to handle a situation such as a raid. If you are new and haven't done anything like this before, first of all you shouldn't be working alone ever; but even more so then. Make sure the agent you are working with knows what is going on and ask questions of the law enforcement agency that is assisting you, explain to them you are just trying to learn their technique so you may implement it into your procedures. Never be embarrassed and afraid to express your thoughts and opinions on any situation and ask questions if you don't understand, if you don't understand you could be putting yourself or the people with you at risk of injury.

Don't act like a know it all either, I have traveled all over the USA as an agent and have had something to learn from everyone I have worked with; and by no means have I ever claimed to be an expert in the field I worked in because that is an awfully broad title to bestow upon anyone, especially in this field as it is always changing.

The one thing I have been aware of in this type of industry is that there is never anyone who can know everything about this type of work, any good academy will tell you they are teaching you the current up to date laws but that they are changing all the time and it is your responsibility to check into the laws yourself and to familiarize yourself with the location to find these laws and their updates periodically. A good agent will research laws for the states he/she is operating in at least once a month and especially if going out of state for a case he/she will be sure to research laws in that state before conducting an investigation.

Always be open to learning from anyone and everyone, I have worked on cases where the fugitive has explained to me how they did their crime or how they have gotten away with things in the past; take things into consideration and make notes of it and share it with others.

DEALING WITH THE MEDIA

Dealing with the media is something you may not have to do but in case it is offered or assigned here are some basic ideas and things to remember when dealing with the media.

Always state what your rules are and get it in writing that the media will follow those rules or legal action will be taken to ensure that these rules are followed expressly.

Always be polite and know what you are talking about. If don't know the answer to a question advise the person that you will look into that for them and get back to them as soon as possible.

If they are filming you in the course of your duties act professional!!! Do not use profanity or use excessive force (you should never do these things anyways), and explain what you are doing and why you are doing it. This will be appreciated and it will help you look more like a professional and that is what you want to be portrayed as no matter what.

Try not to hesitate during the interview or coverage. Hesitation shows incompetence and is never very professional.

Make sure you stress the importance of how laws are dictated and presented as well as how your authority and power of arrest is depicted, you want to give the public a proper understanding of industry.

Don't be an actor! There are numerous television shows and movies depicting bounty hunters in an awful way and all it does is cause problems for anyone who is employed in this industry when someone acts instead of depicting how things really are.

Show them the whole shebang. That means showing them all the work that goes into solving a case and not just the glorified arrest itself, show them it takes skill and precision to apprehend the fugitive and it is not as easy as people think it is.

Stress the importance of training and the legitimacy of training and what the difference is between a trained recovery agent and someone who isn't trained. Be sure to include where you attended your academy and if you were satisfied with your training mention that as well; your academy will appreciate it and you never know it might help you get some work from that academy.

Don't hog the spotlight!!!! And sure to include your partner and/or your team is everything. No person can do it all alone and it's up to you to show them that it is a team effort and that everyone plays a key role.

Always keep a copy of the media related article or story and use it in your advertising campaign. Plus it will be nice to look back on it in future.

GETTING HURT ON THE JOB

It will happen one time or another your going to get hurt while working. Here are some details to help you out along the way so that you may make the best out of the situation.

If you're injured to the point you need medical care immediately call an ambulance! Do not drive yourself to the Emergency Room, the more documentation you have the better. Also if it is an injury directly resulting from an arrest request a police officer to come to the hospital to take a report, that can be a charge against the fugitive and can assist you in getting the medical bill paid for. If it is an injury that does not require immediate assistance, but could need medical assistance go see your family doctor but document that it was related to an arrest made.

Always work with a partner, and make sure both of you are current in your CPR/Advanced First Aid Certification. Keep a well stocked First Aid Kit with you when you work! If you are an EMT or Medic than invest in a jump bag to keep with you when you work, never know when it will come in handy.

Just be careful and be safe, but if something should happen don't be stubborn get it checked out, you don't want to be laid up if you don't have to be.

GETTING A CONTRACT

Getting the contract with the bondsman is what will get you work so obviously you'll want to do it right. So let's get started! Not everyone has good business sense so I will cover what you need to do to get business and if you're a business type run with it!

First of all you need to put on paper what to do, be professional yet short, bondsman are very busy and they get hundreds of these every month so say something to catch their eye. Also include a resume and in your cover letter tell them why they should pick you. Former law enforcement or military tends to get the most attention but let them know by your appearance and by your paperwork that your not a gung ho GI JOE or SWAT guy and you know what the tasks of the job are. Also a photo of you to go with paperwork is always a good idea that gives the bondsman a chance to put the paperwork with a face. Make sure it is a professional photo maybe of you in a shirt and tie or other appropriate apparel. If your going into the bondsman's office here's what to wear, either a dress shirt open collar or polo shirt and khakis or dress pants, NEVER JEANS AND A T-SHIRT OR SWAT GET UP!! You want to be taken seriously not laughed at or shunned away. Always follow up within 2-3 days of dropping it off or if mailing it out within a week with a phone call. Remember if you are going in person shake his or her hand firmly and professionally, always look them in the eye and never hesitate that shows incompetence.

Second of all you need to not just focus on the bondsman in your area but bondsman in the surrounding states to start off and you need to make sure you do follow up calls! Keep calling one of two things will happen they will tell you to screw off or they will give you a case. Be stern on your price!!! If you budge on your price that shows them that your not grounded and that shows more incompetence, the only way you should budge on price is if you have a pre set arrangement made with the bondsman. Generally what you get is 10% of the bail bond amount NEVER settle for anything less than $250 and make this known to the bondsman up front! Once you get good at what you do and the bondsman gets to know you and your abilities you can get 10% in state and 15-20% out of state and sometimes even expenses to an extent. I had great deals worked out with bondsman and I made good amount of money doing it.

I highly recommend joining as many associations as possible, I know I bitched about them but there are some that I recommend because I have gotten work from them. One in particular is the United States Professional Bail Bond Investigators Association (www.bountyhunt.com) they will issue you a control number and ID, Certificate and T-Shirt for only $45 a year! It's a great deal and you get some good stuff, plus Billy Wells the founder and head of the USPBIA is always there to help new agents out. An invaluable expense. Also you can try other associations just look on the internet and you'll find them, check them out before joining and good luck.

LEGAL ISSUES

With the rise of lawsuits in our industry the last thing you need is a sexual harassment suit or any type of sexual misconduct suit against you so act professional. I have worked many cases where either the fugitive or someone directly related to the case was very attractive and even the simplest flirtatious gesture can cost you your job and a lot of money. So when your out there, be careful of how you act, again you never know who is watching you or who is out to get you. If a prisoner ever offers you sexual favors for her or his release be sure to log it down in the report and advise the correctional officer what was said upon arriving at the jail, remember paperwork, paperwork, paperwork. Document everything, if your ever wrongly accused of misconduct as long as you are truthful and have good documentation you shouldn't have any problems. Listen to the agents you work with that have done this for a while, they will show you and tell you how to handle the situations that will come up. NEVER be alone with someone of the opposite sex during an investigation! Whether it be someone your interviewing or the fugitive themselves be aware this is a society that is all about the almighty dollar, so everyone is out to make money at the other persons expense.

Again I recommend retaining the services of Pre Paid Legal or a like program where you have access to an attorney wherever you may be. This service will prove to be an invaluable tool throughout your career and offers counseling services as well when you have legal questions. I have personally used the services of an attorney prior to testifying in a case, when falsely sued for being too aggressive and other situations where it warranted legal advice.

Be smart, Be professional and you shouldn't have any problems; but should the need arise be prepared! Always have good documentation of your case and be sure that the client has a complete copy of the file as well.

COMMON SENSE

Well first of all I have lived by this quote as much to my ability as possible.

" LOYALTY ABOVE ALL ELSE EXCEPT HONOR "

That is a pretty bold and meaningful statement to live by let me tell you. What it means is that you will be loyal and trusting unless what is going on or being said is not honorable and could damage the credibility of you, your staff and the agency you represent. Again, remember this is a business of lessening liability and the name of the game is to save the bondsman money.

Look at it from this point of view; you're an insurance investigator with the power of arrest, because essentially that is the truth. The bail bond is insuring that the defendant will appear in court and the bondsman is putting up the money to secure that, when the defendant fails to appear in court as scheduled then you are required to investigate and apprehend that person to be turned into the jail so that the bondsman will be cleared of responsibility of the defendant.

Always portray a positive self image both on and off duty, you never know who is watching you and who it could back to. Be careful of who you cross in this business, all it takes is one person saying you're a cowboy or that you are not doing a good job and that could be the end of your career as a fugitive recovery agent. Also remember this is a "cut throat" business and everyone is in it to make money. Remember you can learn from everyone, when I was teaching future agents I learned a lot from them, some were from corrections and I learned new and innovative techniques not available to the private sector and I implemented that into my training till I had it down and was good at it, there may be a private investigator you work for that can teach you to be a master at surveillance, maybe a police officer teaching you how to interview someone; whatever the case be open to learning from everyone, you will be a better agent doing so.

Men, when it comes to surveillance or a time when you can't get out of the vehicle, use a wide mouth soda bottle or sports drink bottle to urinate in. My best advice for going number 2 is to do it before you head out and be careful what you eat! The worst thing in the world is stuck in a car doing surveillance during the cold of winter and someone breaking wind and not being able to roll down the window because of the cold and snow, "courtesy counts, mother f*&cker" a wise man named Stone once said.

What you should have in your gear bag. Like I said at least 2 days worth of changes of clothes appropriate for the season, hygiene products, a well stocked First Aid Kit, at least 4 bottles of water (brushing teeth, drinking water and whatever else you might need it for), MRE's (Meals Ready to Eat) are a great resource especially when you know you might be stuck in the car for a while, Aspirin or likewise medication for headaches or joint aches, stomach settler like Pepto or something like that you'll need eventually trust me, especially true in winter months is a need for a good light blanket (I recommend a military wool blanket and a campers pillow). Whatever you may think you might need throw it in there, never know when you'll need it.

TRUTH ABOUT THIS JOB

Well this is the part I hate to talk about but it is only fair that you know the truth before you get into this job and get stuck and lose everything. This is a job of dedication and inconvenience and you never know when you're going to get a call to work. I have been pulled away from family events, been paged out of church and have been in bed with my wife when a page went off. So as you can see anywhere anytime you can get called to serve your client. This is especially true when you work for an agency and they are expecting you to work all the time, don't even consider getting a day off, in this job there are no days off. Some of the busiest times of the year are Christmas Eve and Christmas Day, Mothers' Day and Easter. I know these days are usually reserved for family, but once you work this job long enough you will see these are money days when you make multiple arrests if you have multiple open cases.

I know agents who have lost their families due to the demands of this job, this is where common sense and order comes in. I used to work anywhere from 6am to 3am 7 days a week and it burned me out real quick so I developed a schedule, when I did work a case I would devote as much time as possible and work as many hours as possible but employed other agents to work with me so that the stress of a lot of the field work was taken off of me and I could do more family related activities. Although I have been married 5 times and have 6 children, I know I did not devote the time I should have in my marriages and the fact that I recognize that now is obviously too late but a worthy note. Life is hard as it is, and this job will make it harder. Your weight will fluctuate and you will get run down worse than you ever imagined. You will learn to sleep anywhere and 20-30 minute naps will serve as your daily amount of sleep on occasion. Even when you are off duty (when you have an open case your never off duty) you will catch yourself checking everyone and more and more people will began to look like your fugitive. You will learn that sleeping at home in your comfortable bed is a privilege only granted when you have exhausted all your efforts working the case. It sounds horrible but its manageable and eventually you will learn that it is a way of life for the professional agent.

I tell all single agents that I have worked with if you learn to balance a social life with your career that's great and more power to you. But if your married with young children be careful, time flies by quickly and you will regret this job and resent it so learn to balance your life with it.

My contact information is in your hand and in this publication, contact me anytime I will be more than happy to assist you in anyway I can.

Something that most people don't realize is that this job is a job that requires skill, it's not something you can be taught in a classroom in one weekend, that only gets you the basics. It's something you learn along the way through experience. Many have tried in this industry and failed and the biggest complaint I have heard was that they invested too much money in the beginning and went into debt. I can't stress enough that you should not spend a lot of money in the beginning, only get the essentials and from there you will accumulate the gear and equipment you want over time.

One of my few faults in this business is I did not hear what seasoned agents were telling me, I listened but I was young and arrogant and didn't want someone telling me what to do. Trust me, you need to listen and HEAR what they tell you; they have a lot to offer in the way of knowledge and they can be very helpful and you never know a tip from one of them may help you solve a case.

Again, you have two ears and one mouth, if you listen twice as much as you talk you may learn something. One of my favorite theologians Og Mandino said " I once felt bad for a man who had no shoes, then I met a man who had no feet " Think about that statement, things are never as bad as they seem and can only get better. It may seem hopeless when you first start out but as you grow in this business so will your reputation and before you now it you will have steady work coming in. Just be persistent!!! Don't give up on the job and it won't give up on you. Naturally there are some people that end up realizing they are just not cut out for this job, but only you can figure that out on your own. Are you a wolf or a sheep?

I have worked with agents from 18-60 years old, each of them have taught me something about this job in one way or the other; maybe a way of investigating or a way of interrogating someone. The point is, skill is something that you can pick up from anywhere and anyone, not just from a classroom environment. There are all types of books that can help you along the way, from Interviewing to advanced tactics, our company store sells them, contact me if you are interested in learning more. As always I recommend you take advanced classes, whether it be with ODBH Services or another reputable firm, never stop learning!

This job is like playing chess, it's a strategic mind game and one wrong move could cost you the game. Just like one wrong move you can lose your fugitive, it's really up to you; you must learn to apply your skills to better yourself and your colleagues.

DON'T BE A HERO

DON'T BE A HERO!!!! It's not your job to go bursting in like the police do and try and save the day, leave it to the police to do their job and focus on your job catching your fugitive.

Remember the police once they engage and attempt to subdue someone have to stay there and get it done, not a recovery agent! You can leave and come back another day; personally I don't know anyone who has ever left a fugitive and came back, but the option is there nonetheless.

If your fugitive has a weapon, don't try and be a hero and take it from him or her unless it's a last resort tactic. Hopefully you will have the assistance of local police and they will assist you in getting your fugitive into custody; but if not, be smart and use your head, try and talk them down from doing anything stupid, this is where I recommend use of a Taser or likewise application of force.

EXPENSES

Probably one of the most important things that will be of concern to you as an agent is expenses. Expenses can make or break you, I will tell you how to keep them low and utilize the tax write off system to gain your money back. You are an Independent Contractor so all your expenses are a write off.

When you buy new equipment no matter how cheap or expensive SAVE THE RECEIPT! Keep it in a folder marked with each calendar month and type of expense it is. At the end of the year take this to your accountant and they will tally up your write offs and you will get a nice check back or maybe break even. Now remember your job requires you to have a vast array of clothing and equipment and some things may cost you $ 10.00, while others cost in excess of $ 1,000.00. Everything from clothing to your cell phone bill each month, make a copy and highlight each of the calls used in your duty and you can use it to write off. ALWAYS get a gas receipt when working! As well as refreshments and food too! Parking receipts, toll booths everything and anything that you spend money on while working you can use the receipts for taxes.

Again, I talked about the importance of business cards and the importance of them looking professional, if you have the skills and the print program you can buy blank business card sheets and print your own, I suggest this for dealing with informants and the public, but get some professionally made for dealing with bondsman and law enforcement.

One thing you will go through a lot of is ink for your printer, if your printer allows it get the refill kits they will save you a lot of money; if your going to use a store that specializes in business supplies (I HIGHLY RECOMMEND THIS) then sign up for their rewards programs so that you can save even more money. Your trying to do your job with the least amount of overhead expenses as possible.

When working you will want to have plenty of the following at all times: BLACK ink pens, paperclips and stapler, at least 3 legal pads, and small pocket sized notebooks for taking notes. KEEP ALL YOUR NOTES! NEVER KNOW WHEN THEY WIL BE SUBPOENAED!

I also recommend getting a separate phone line or evoice mail setup registered to your business name. It will give more legitimacy to the operation and will save you money on your cell phone minutes.

Regular internet won't cut it, go and by a wireless card and use that service for your laptop as it can go wherever you go.

PHYSICAL'S, SHOTS AND DOCTORS VISITS

First thing is you need to get your hepatitis shot! With everything going around these days it's better to be safe than sorry. Also since you will be working in inclement weather you'll want to get a flu shot as well.

You will want to advise your family doctor on what type of work you are doing, and if you have any special needs he can best route you to the appropriate treatment to help; such as knee braces, anti-inflammatory etc. You need vitamins everyday, no joke, get Flintstones Chewables, they are good and they will help especially when you get used to working long hours.

Contacts instead of glasses, last thing you want is to have your vision screwed up by fogging glasses. They cost about the same as glasses do and are more convenient.

Get a physical from your family doctor every 6 months. Always be honest with him and let him know of any significant problems or concerns that may arise.

If traumatic events occur such as a death or accident while working, get counseling. It may seem you don't need it at the time but it will benefit you in the long run and Post Traumatic Stress is a common problem in the private sector field today and should be taken seriously as it will only result in you losing your reputation and your functioning skills as an agent without proper care.

If you get hurt in the line of duty, don't be so quick to rush back; take your time and heal be sure that you are as close to 100% as possible before returning to work. Don't risk yours or your partners life because of pride it's not worth it.

OPPORTUNITY KNOCKS, LET IT IN!!!

Once you start doing this job you will realize it opens up avenues for other work in the private sector. I always told my students NEVER quit your full time job, always do this part time until you are established enough and have a steady income coming in. I have seen a lot of agents crash and burn for not listening to that piece of advice.

- **SERVICE OF PROCESS** - In some states anyone 18 or older of sound mind and judgment can serve process, chances are an attorney or court is going to want someone who is a good investigator in case the person needing to be served is a hard to find individual. Plus if the person you serve contests the serve you want to know what your talking about and be professional as this will make or break the case. Just like in a arrest report you need to describe what the person looked like, was wearing and an identifying characteristic that would charge your memory to identify the person in court.
- **PRIVATE INVESTIGATION** - Although most states require a license to perform this job; you can work as a freelance P.I. under someone else's license just paying them a small fee to hold your licensing. Remember if you are not working under a license the investigation report will not hold up in court.

Remember ethics in everything you do, if you have a bad feeling that it isn't right what your doing then don't do it. YOU HAVE THE RIGHT to question any practices that you deem unfit, especially if it could result in legal action upon you so use your head and be smart about things.

- **EXECUTIVE/DIGNITARY PROTECTION** - There are several well established recovery agents that also provide executive protection services. Most of them are not properly trained in Executive Protection Protocol and are generally the huge guys that are "protecting" the celebrities. If you want to be taken serious in the protection industry your not 6'5", 350 Lbs wearing a tight t shirt and black dress pants. A true professional protection agent is someone who is not obvious but very alert, someone who dresses for the environment. So if this is another avenue I suggest you take it seriously and get the training, there is more than enough work out there in this field for true professionals.

LOSS PREVENTION - This is an interesting way of providing security, investigating and apprehending retail theft offenders at stores. Every major retailer and grocer has L.P. "Store Detectives" who wear plainclothes and investigate internal and external theft problems like catching shoplifters, this is a good way to build up your experience as an investigator and generally a good way to make a living. Try it out, I made a part time job out of it for a few years during down time. And the level of investigator I was afterwards was totally different and much more successful afterwards.

SECURITY OFFICER - There is a difference between "Security Guard and Security Officer". An officer is a professional, neat, trained OFFICER; a guard is a $ 5.00 an hour body to stand post. Get with a good company and take as much training as possible, hey it will help pay the bills and strengthen your skills as an agent. Some places require licensing to be a Security Agent, add that to your resume it's worth the time.

REPOSSESSION AGENT - The infamous, "REPO MAN". I too did this job and loved it! What could be more fun then stealing cars legally for a living? Seriously though it's great money making anywhere from $ 50-$350 per vehicle your recover. I have worked for agencies where I used a pick up truck with a boom and I have worked for agencies where I simply walked up to the door and demanded the car, I prefer using a truck and getting the car in the middle of the night or while they are at work, etc. I would incorporate into your business this service, and it is a lucrative income.

Whatever else you do is fine too. I know guys that are full time computer technicians and do recovery on their time off, I have known Firefighters to Nurses who have done this as a "Hobby". One guy I worked with was a pilot and had his own plane, and when he had a run out of state he would just transport his fugitive via plane and get the local Police to pick them up at the airport. There are a vast array of careers that can help you gain skill in your business, it's up to you to make the right decisions to make your recovery business work.

FIELD WORK

Once you have done your work at home you will have to go into the field sometime in your investigation. When you do dress comfortable but professional. Jeans and a polo, or cargo khakis and a button down, etc. Draw as little attention to yourself as possible! Be stern and do not back down if you know there is something more behind what you are seeing. A good investigator can take notes while interviewing the person and make them feel comfortable, remember to jot down everything you never know what is going to be needed and what is not, some of the dumbest answers to questions have solved my cases.

When you go into a residence, take notice of the things around you. Pictures, décor things that you can use to "bullshit" with them and get them to open up to you. If going into a business, dress professional and be personable but not flirtatious, get what you came for and always thank them.

Any more details would be doing your job for you!

Now, everyone has their own ways of conducting interviews and interrogations, NEVER THREATEN THE PERSON WITH HARM!!!! You can threaten them legally with such things as hindering an apprehension, aiding and abetting, harboring a fugitive, defrauding an insurance company etc. But always try the comfortable , nice routine first.

When I worked as a Process Service Officer in Detroit, my Chief taught me a valuable lesson. "Use your instinct and know your environment" That teaching has never left me and never been more of a true statement, trust your instincts! If you have a bad feeling chances are your right on the money. I have worked in some of the roughest neighborhoods of the world and some of the wealthiest neighborhoods, and the one thing I have learned the most is NO ONE wants to be a "rat" and tell you where your fugitive is, or give information. That's when you use your skills to persuade them and develop confidential informants which I have already covered.

HYGEINE AND APPEARANCE

First of all there are many different ways to style your hair as we all know, but come on use common sense does long hair all shaggy and a ripped up shirt look professional? Of course not, and if you want to be taken seriously dress for success.

Men, keep your hair trimmed and professional no ponytails and all that crap, your not on TV. and this is real life not scripted so act like it.

Women, I always recommend that hair be kept pulled up or cut short, this is for safety reasons as well as to look neat. The same thing applies to women and men with regards to hair, most female agents I have dealt with wear a ball cap as well as the men especially in the winter months.

Facial hair should ALWAYS be kept neat and trimmed and not look raggedy. Remember you are a profession and want to be perceived as a professional not just in your clothing but in your physical appearance.

Dress for the season you are in. Never wear shorts at anytime when working as an agent, it just isn't safe at all and looks unprofessional.

Since you will be carrying a lot of things to assist you, I always recommend cargo khakis if you plan on wearing khakis, I will again promote the famous 5.11 series as the best in the world. But remember at any time you may get into a brawl or a chase, be prepared to get dirty and/or clothes torn up at one time or another.

ALWAYS HAVE DEODORANT WITH YOU AND USE IT!!!!! Remember you don't want to offend. But do not douse yourself in cologne either as you don't want to give anyone a headache.

ALWAYS CARRY BREATH MINTS!!!! The last thing you want to do is offend someone with your breath as you will realize you will be in a lot of conversations while working.

Dress for the environment as you will understand that you will be accepted a lot easier if you look like you belong in that particular environment. This is especially true when working in a business setting where you will want to be in business casual or shirt and tie, whatever you feel necessary for the job at hand. I personally always have a polo on, and switch from jeans to tactical pants khaki colors, always keep a neutral color sports coat with you in case you are needing to adapt to a more classy environment. Just a few ideas to help you along the way that worked for me. A good agent is prepared for anything to happen and expects the worse every time he goes out but prays for the easiest outcome.

BASIC PRISONER PROCESSING

Prisoner Processing is an important factor in your job as it will happen 100% of the time when you surrender your fugitive to the jail. I am going to cover just a few things that are important during this process that you need to know.

- BE POLITE. Chances are most of the corrections officers are going to ask you a lot of questions about what you do because they have a genuine interest in your field. As for the questions, they will also come because they may have never dealt with a recovery agent before so be prepared and be open to questions and be sure to give them business cards should they have any further questions.
- BE IN ORDER. One thing that will upset the corrections staff is the arresting agent not having paperwork in order! When you surrender the defendant to the jail you need to have the following documents readily available for viewing: A copy of warrant if applicable, copy of authorization to arrest, copy of bail bond agreement. Also have your report handy so the receiving corrections officer can sign off custody and always get a body receipt when available or some proof you brought them in!
- SECURE YOUR WEAPONS AND KEYS! Make sure you secure your weapons and your car keys in the locker provided at the sally port when surrendering your prisoner. This is for safety reasons and is required for all agents/officers entering the facility. NEVER EVER FORGET THIS!!!
- Wait till agents have secured their weapons and keys in the locker then get prisoner out of vehicle and take him into jail. Once there you should have a property bag with all items that were on the defendant at time of arrest. The corrections officer will then search the subject again and enter him into the processing area for booking. You can then show the paperwork to the corrections officer and get it signed to relieve you of custody.
- COMPLETE YOUR REPORT AT THE Jail!!! After you surrender your prisoner and leave the sally port, go to the parking lot no matter what time it is and finish your report while everything is still fresh in your head. Make sure to include any incidents such as use of force or anything relating to the arrest that may be needed for court. And as always have a typed and a copy of the original report to the client the next business day.

USING UNIVERSAL PRECAUTIONS

Using the Universal Precautions rules mean never being exposed to any blood born pathogens or bodily fluids due to the overwhelming number of diseases going throughout the world today especially in the United States.

The first rule of any arrest is to wear protective gloves, I always recommend a pair of batting gloves so when searching you can feel and they are thin enough to feel strong enough to protect.

ALWAYS! Disinfect your equipment that touches the fugitive. I recommend using alcohol and wiping down your gloves, handcuffs and leg irons. Also, if by any chance you get blood or other bodily fluid on your equipment use bleach to disinfect the equipment.

If the prisoner starts spitting on you, simply pull the front of their shirt over their face or keep a dark colored pillowcase and bag them.

If you know there is a communicable disease present be sure to take appropriate action and notify corrections staff right away.

* If you are ever injured, poked by a needle or come into contact with someone else's bodily fluid, wash area thoroughly first and then go to the emergency room as soon as possible to get checked out.

BE SAFE, BE SMART AND IT'S NOT ALWAYS EASY BUT MAKE EVERY EFFORT TO BE SAFE.

CODE OF ETHICS

- TO PERFORM ALL FUGITIVE INVESTIGATIONS IN A MORAL, ETHICAL AND LEGAL MANNER.
- TO ARREST THE FUGITIVE IN THE MOST HUMANE, LEGAL AND RESPONSIBLE MANNER POSSIBLE.
- TO WORK ENTIRELY WITHIN THE FRAMEWORK OF THE LAW; LOCAL STATE AND FEDERAL.
- TO VERIFY ALL PAPERWORK, WARRANTS AND DOCUMENTS THAT MAY LEAD TO A WRONGFUL ARREST OR DETENTION.
- TO ACT IN A FASHION TO BRING CREDIT IN THE AGENCY YOU REPERESENT.
- TO REPORT ALL FACTS AND DEVELOPMENTS IN THE CASE PROMPTLY AND TIMELY IN ORDER TO ASSIST THE AGENCY YOU REPRESENT.
- TO MAINTAIN A HIGHLY TRAINED TEAM OF AGENTS THAT ARE SKILLED AND MOTIVATED.
- TO KEEP INFORMED OF ALL CHANGES I THE FUGITIVE RECOVERY INDUSTRY.
- TO MAINTAIN A PROFESSIONAL WORKING RELATIONSHIP WITH ALL LOCAL, STATE AND FEDERAL LAW ENFORCEMENT AGENCIES.
- TO BE READY TO OPERATE ANYTIME, ANYWHERE AND UNDER ANY SITUATION.

These are the guidelines I personally was issued in 1998. Although we all try to abide by these codes, it is seldom possible in today's society.

BREAKING INTO THE HOUSE FOR THAT PURPOSE

While I never recommend breaking down a door or picking a lock to get into the home of a fugitive to make the arrest, there may come a time when you don't have a choice. Taylor v Taintor as we previously discussed gives you the authority to do so.

FIRST, always knock hard as you can announce yourself loudly BAIL ENFORCEMENT OPEN THE DOOR!!!! Use your judgment, if the defendant is in the house and you know it force your way in, keep yelling BAIL ENFORCEMENT as you walk through the home. More than likely you will have the police there as backup and they will be assisting you in the arrest and forced entry.

This is short but just remember what we went over in the class. Any questions call or email me.

ENDING NOTES

Many will say you don't need a badge, their right; but if you want to be taken seriously get one. Never use a badge that in anyway looks or says anything about law enforcement agencies. There are several "generic" badges that you can use, the one issued to you during this course has been in my opinion the most professional badge for our industry ever produced.

YOU MUST HAVE CREDENTIALS!!!! There are many companies out there that will sell generic style credentials for recovery agents. You will need to remember these are your professional ID's so look professional in the photo.

Your not a cop, remember that. No bonding agent wants to see a SWAT wannabe walk into their office, although there may be times when this type of look is warranted, more likely you will be in plainclothes.

Body armor is an invaluable tool! Yes they are expensive, but so is a funeral. I recommend a level IIA concealable vest that you can wear year round. I am able to get Level IIIA Vests with TRAUMA PACK for $ 375.00 With shipping. Contact me for details.

Business cards, go to www.vistaprint.com and the possibilities are endless. NEVER USE OFFICER, DEPUTY OR ANYTHING LIKE THAT!

If the fugitive is on medication make sure you have it when you arrest them and that the fugitives name is on the container. NO OVER THE COUNTER MEDICATION SHALL BE ADMINSTERED!!! Before transporting begins be sure to ask the fugitive about any medical conditions or medications and be sure to log them all down in your log and report.

ANYTHING ELSE YOU HAVE QUESTIONS ABOUT CONTACT ME AT:

Odbhservices@yahoo.com

Or call (314) 308-3346 or Text

ABOUT THE AUTHOR

Kelly Cresswell has been involved in the private sector field since 1998, has assisted in the apprehension of over 2500 fleeing felony fugitives and countless misdemeanor cases. Kelly has worked in the capacity of PRIVATE MILITARY CONTRACTOR, EXECUTIVE/DIGNITARY PROTECTION AGENT, LOSS PREVENTION DETECTIVE, PRIVATE INVESTIGATOR, SPECIAL COURT OFFICER, REPOSSESSION AGENT AND INTELLIGENCE OPERATIVE/ANALYST.

Kelly has completed thousands of hours of training worldwide in his respective fields, and is considered amongst the bail industry as an expert in the field of bail fugitive investigations.

FACEBOOK:
Boondocksaintkelly
EMAIL:
Boondocksaintkelly@yahoo.com

Made in the USA
San Bernardino, CA
14 August 2020